To Isha D.S.

To Lin G.B.

Copyright © Text Dyan Sheldon 1990
Copyright © Illustrations Gary Blythe 1990

The rights of Dyan Sheldon and Gary Blythe to be identified as
the author and illustrator of this work have been asserted by
them in accordance with the Copyright, Designs and Patents Act,
1988.

First published in 1990 by Hutchinson Children's Books
an imprint of the Random Century Group Ltd
20 Vauxhall Bridge Road, London SW1V 2SA

Random Century Australia (Pty) Ltd
20 Alfred Street, Milsons Point, Sydney, NSW 2061

Random Century New Zealand Ltd
PO Box 40-086, Glenfield, Auckland 10, New Zealand

Random Century South Africa (Pty) Ltd
PO Box 337, Bergvlei, 2012, South Africa

Designed by Paul Welti
Set in Perpetua by Spectrum Typesetting, London
Colour separation by Wace Ltd, London
Printed in Great Britain by Jolly and Barber Ltd, Rugby
Bound by Maclehose Ltd, Portsmouth

British Library Cataloguing in Publication Data
Sheldon, Dyan
The whales' song
I. Title   II. Blythe, Gary
813.54 (J)

ISBN 0-09-174250-1

THE WHALES' SONG

Story by Dyan Sheldon

Illustrations by Gary Blythe

HUTCHINSON

London Sydney Auckland Johannesburg

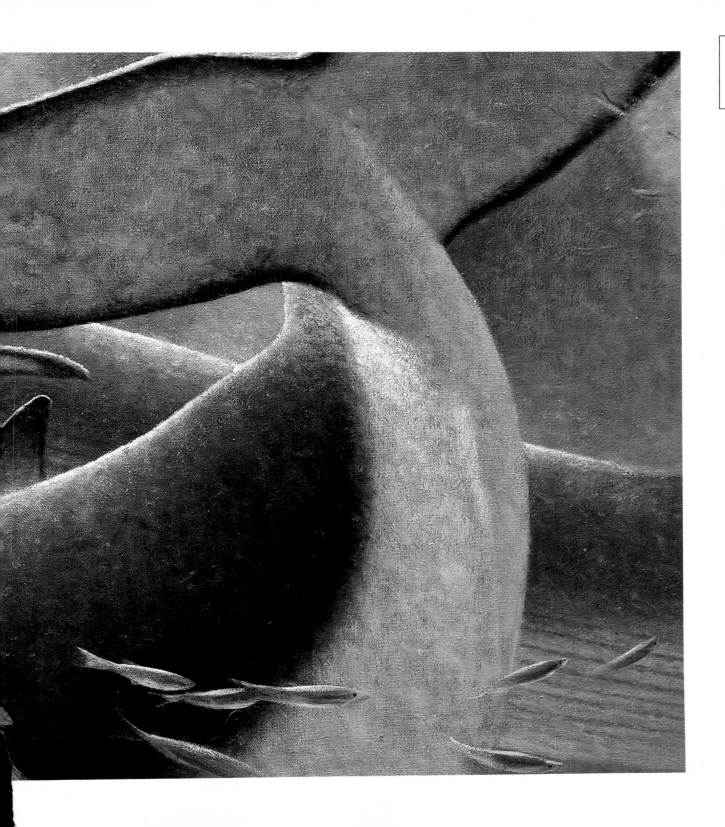

ILLY'S grandmother told her a story.

'Once upon a time,' she said, 'the ocean was filled with whales. They were as big as the hills. They were as peaceful as the moon. They were the most wondrous creatures you could ever imagine.'

*L*ILLY climbed on to her grandmother's lap.

'I used to sit at the end of the jetty and listen for whales,' said Lilly's grandmother. 'Sometimes I'd sit there all day and all night. Then all of a sudden I'd see them coming from miles away. They moved through the water as if they were dancing.'

'*B*UT how did they know you were there, Grandma?' asked Lilly. 'How would they find you?'

Lilly's grandmother smiled. 'Oh, you had to bring them something special. A perfect shell. Or a beautiful stone. And if they liked you the whales would take your gift and give you something in return.'

'**W**HAT would they give you, Grandma?' asked Lilly. 'What did you get from the whales?'

Lilly's grandmother sighed. 'Once or twice,' she whispered, 'once or twice I heard them sing.'

*L*ILLY's uncle Frederick stomped into the room. 'You're nothing but a daft old fool!' he snapped. 'Whales were important for their meat, and for their bones, and for their blubber. If you have to tell Lilly something, then tell her something useful. Don't fill her head with nonsense. Singing whales indeed!'

'THERE were whales here millions of years before there were ships, or cities, or even cavemen,' continued Lilly's grandmother. 'People used to say they were magical.'

'People used to eat them and boil them down for oil!' grumbled Lilly's uncle Frederick. And he turned his back and stomped out to the garden.

*L*ILLY dreamt about whales.

In her dreams she saw them, as large as mountains and bluer than the sky. In her dreams she heard them singing, their voices like the wind. In her dreams they leapt from the water and called her name.

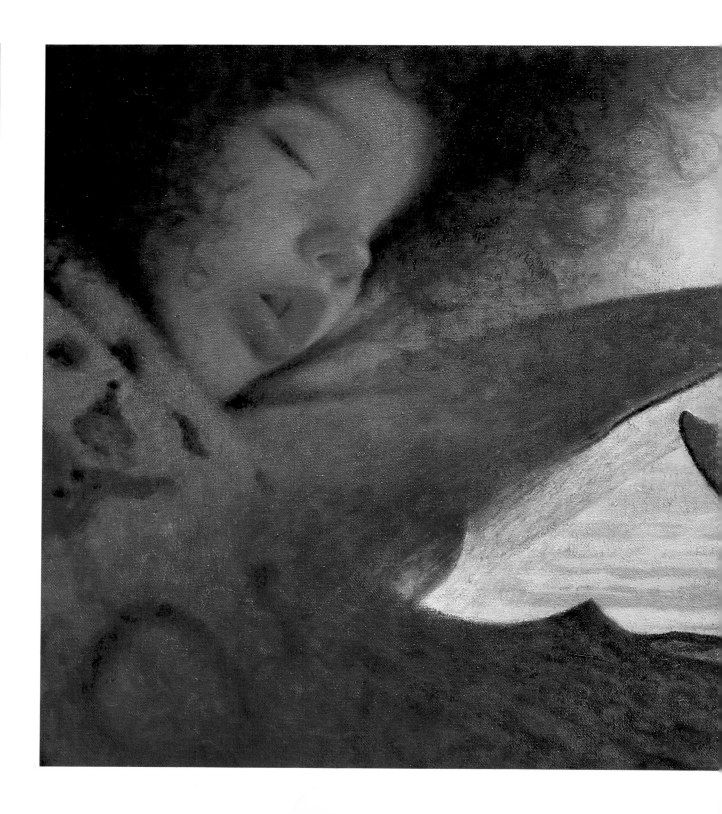

N ext morning Lilly went down to the ocean. She went where no one fished or swam or sailed their boats. She walked to the end of the old jetty, the water was empty and still. Out of her pocket she took a yellow flower and dropped it in the water.

'This is for you,' she called into the air.

*L*ILLY sat at the end of the jetty and waited.

She waited all morning and all afternoon.

Then, as dusk began to fall, Uncle Frederick came down the hill after her. 'Enough of this foolishness,' he said. 'Come on home. I'll not have you dreaming your life away.'

*T*HAT night, Lilly awoke suddenly.

The room was bright with moonlight. She sat up and listened. The house was quiet. Lilly climbed out of bed and went to the window. She could hear something in the distance, on the far side of the hill.

S HE raced outside
and down to the shore.
Her heart was pounding
as she reached the sea.

There enormous in the
ocean, were the whales.

They leapt and jumped
and spun across the moon.

Their singing filled up
the night.

Lilly saw her yellow
flower dancing on the
spray.

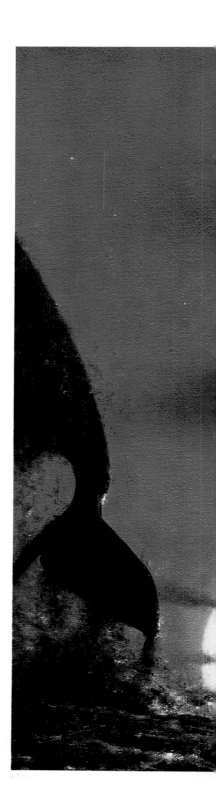

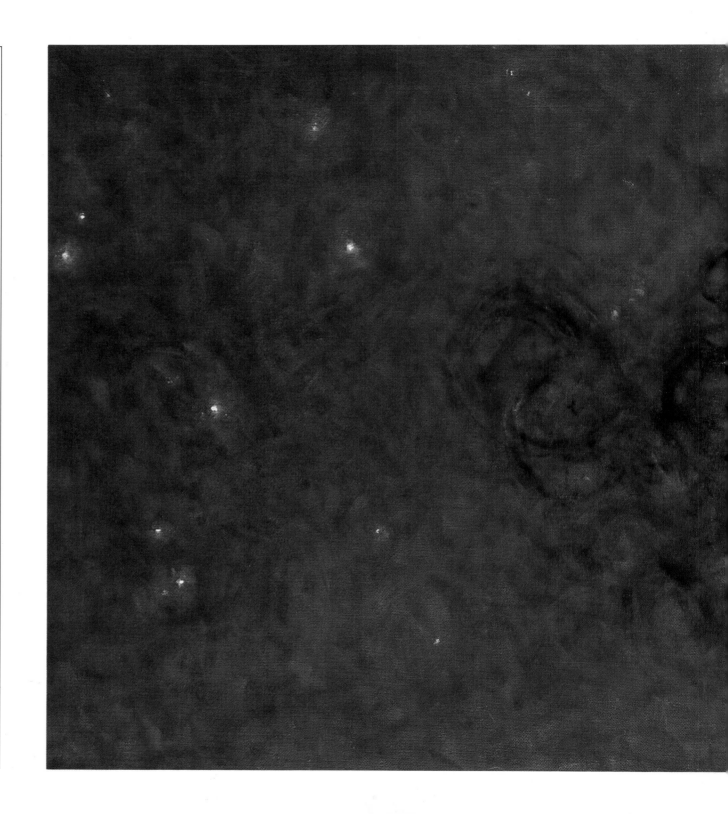

M INUTES passed, or maybe hours. Suddenly Lilly felt the breeze rustle her nightdress and the cold nip at her toes. She shivered and rubbed her eyes. Then it seemed the ocean was still again and the night black and silent.

Lilly thought she must have been dreaming. She stood up and turned for home. Then from far, far away, on the breath of the wind she heard,
'Lilly!
Lilly!'
The whales were calling her name.